# A Very Small Book about a Cabin at Kettle Creek

**Copyright © 2022**

Written by Warren Burda

Illustrated by Elizabeth Carter

## Copyright Disclaimer

*A very small book about a Cabin at Kettle Creek*:
First Edition, Paperback
Publication Date September 2022
Publisher: Alpha Academic Press
ISBN: 978-1-948210-15-7

Alpha
Academic
Press

**Published in the United States of America**

# Acknowledgments

SPECIAL THANKS

to Pastor Erin Morris for the book Introduction

to Mindy West for her help with photographs and layout

to Marion and Ed Boyer for the picture of hiking the logging road

to Elizabeth Carter for her illustrations

and to my wife for encouraging me to do this book

# Dedication

Welcome to A Very Small Book About a Cabin at Kettle Creek. It is based on the twenty-five years that the family spent there. The book is dedicated with much love to the Lord and to the author's parents, now in Heaven, who made those years possible.

My parents at the cabin

# Table of Contents

# A word from the author

I am not ashamed of the Gospel of Jesus Christ! It is the framework from which I wrote this book. The story and characters are imaginary, but everything else is real.

Tom, Judy, TJ, Steve, Michelle, Sara, Dan, and Teri all have one thing in common – at one time or another they spent time at the cabin at Kettle Creek. Each of them struggles to make sense of their lives and faith (so do we), but there is good news. The One who gave us life and the cabin at Kettle Creek holds all of it in His hands. He is continuing to make all things new.

His grace brings those who are willing to the foot of the cross. What happened there makes it possible to be eternally in right relationship with God, to do what pleases Him, to bring light to people in darkness, and to bear good fruit that lasts. But Jesus does not assume what people want, nor does He force it upon them. We find this truth lived out in verse 51 of Mark 10: Then Jesus said to him (a blind beggar named Bartimaeus), "What do you want me to do for you?" The blind man said to Him, "My teacher, let me see again." Jesus healed Bartimaeus physically (his eyes) and spiritually (his heart). The second one is the most important.

Not everyone who prays for physical healing is healed, but anyone who calls upon the name of Jesus, and believes that they have life in His Name are promised that life's difficult days, and the sin and death of this world will not have the final say. It doesn't get any better than that – for the book's characters and for us.

# A Quote

*I went to the woods because I wished to live deliberately,*

*to front only the essential facts of life,*

*and see if I could not learn what it had to teach, and not, when I come*

*to die,*

*discover that I had not lived.*

—Henry David Thoreau, Walden Pond

(This quote was on a green poster in the cabin.

The letters were in white.)

# Introduction

I grew up on over 30 acres of wooded lands. I would spend hours walking, playing, getting "lost" in those woods with my favorite companions, my dogs. It was there that I would speak to Jesus, and He would speak to me through the winds of the Holy Spirit. I felt a sense of peace and calm and connection. Sometimes I would walk through woods and encounter trees that had initials carved into them and I would wonder who was here before me, what the tree had seen, who loved whom, if they were together and so on.

Warren, in his joy for history, family, love and story, takes you on a journey with a cabin by a creek. You will meet various people who have all shared experiences of love and loss in and near the cabin. You will see how their stories are woven, much how God weaves our stories together. You will experience the history of the cabin and the way it brought so many together who would not have met otherwise. And you will see how with love, with hope and with spirit, we are able to experience healing and wholeness.

Enjoy!

Pastor Erin Morris

Associate Pastor, Resurrection Lutheran Church

Oro Valley, AZ

# PART 1 - The Cabin

The cabin was rustic. It was situated a few yards from Kettle Creek on land granted by a 100-year Idaho Forest Service lease. The cabin wasn't much, but it was home to all who stayed in it.

The creek was very small, but it flowed all year and brook trout made it their home. Kids made dams in it, families drank from it, and brushed their teeth in it until giardia made that impossible.

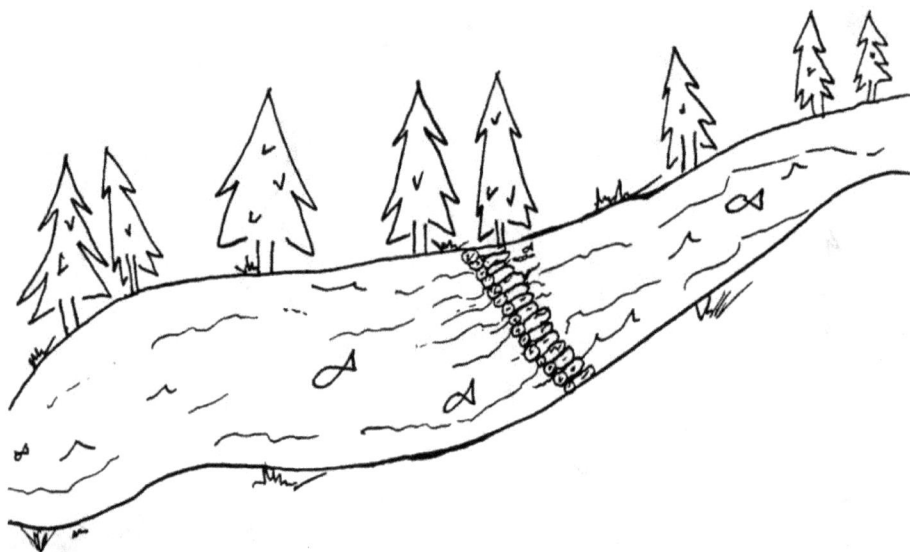

The cabin was break-in proofed. Its five windows were protected by thick wooden coverings that bolted from the inside, and a metal door that hunters occasionally used for target practice.

It had a sink, but only to pour water down. A cast iron stove was used for heating, cooking, and to get an old-style coffee pot percolating in the morning.

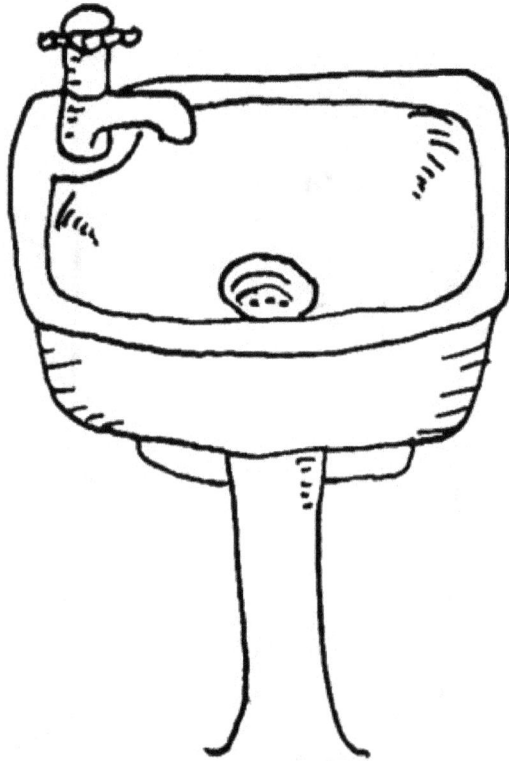

It had one couch that made into a bed and one that didn't. Stairs on the back wall led to a loft with a mattress. It was perfect for gazing at stars through some very tiny holes in the roof, but it made it colder in the morning.

The cabin walls were plain, except for a calendar, a gold mining pan, a green Thoreau poster, Mom's white poster about the earth belonging to God alone, and posters of Uncle Sam and a Vargus Girl.

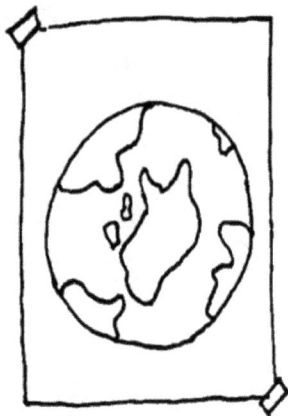

A single light bulb was hung on the ceiling. It was never turned on.

Two lanterns hung over a table with six chairs, providing soft evening light for reading, doing crossword puzzles, or playing scrabble and cards.

Plates, silverware, and coffee cups were stored in a few cupboards and drawers lined with old wallpaper. A postcard was pinned to the inside of a cupboard door.

Wildflowers were made into beautiful bouquets on the cabin table.

A laundry basket was used for keeping drinks cold in the creek.

Wood for the stove was cut with an ax and a double handed saw.

The fishing poles, creoles, and worms were stored against an outside wall of the cabin just to the left of the door.

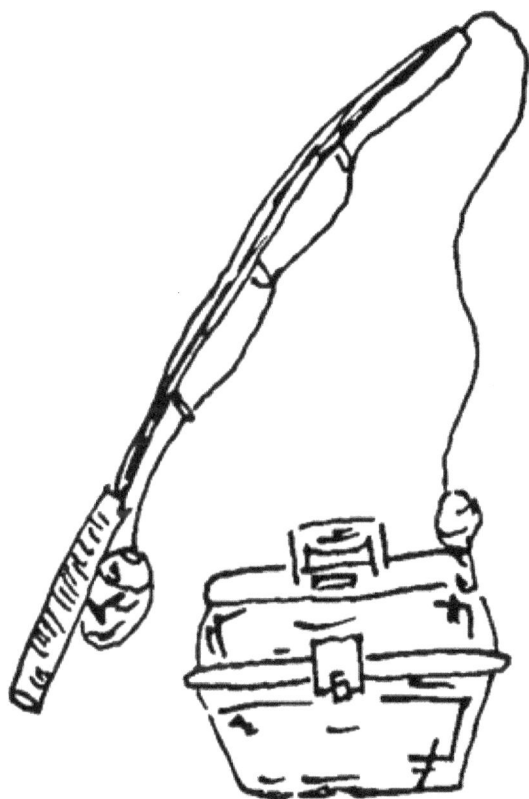

Just above the cabin on the logging road was a salt lick for deer and elk.

In front of the cabin, two lounge chairs and a hammock were used for relaxation.

A wooden picnic table, with a red and white tablecloth, was positioned against the outside cabin wall, a few yards from the creek.

Vehicles were parked in front of the cabin or on either side of the fire pit; leaving room to play lawn darts and throw a tennis ball for the dogs.

In the back of the cabin, a small, abandoned water- powered generator still had some electrical power line hooked to it. An old highway sign lay on the ground next to it.

A few yards down from the cabin door was a rock-lined fire pit.

A few yards up from the cabin was a forest service outhouse, which was decorated inside with a red shower curtain and a Thoreau poster with the different drummer quote.

That was it, except for a small tan wooden box next to the door –
with a notepad and a pencil. Sometimes people left a note, but usually
not.

# PART II - Cafe Couple

*Love .... keeps no record of wrongs.*

1 Corinthians 13: 5

## A little background

Up the road from the cabin at Kettle Creek is the Sourdough Lodge Cafe. It has really good hamburgers, homemade fries, milkshakes, pie, and two-scoop ice cream cones. Besides a really cute eating space, the Sourdough is a hotel and grocery store with a small bar and a pool table. The Sourdough also has two gas pumps and some RV spots. One day, when we were eating lunch there, we couldn't help but look at a couple in a booth across from ours. They were holding hands and looked very much in love.

## Three places of residence

It started as a three-way conference call. This was no small feat to pull off. TJ's dad left his mom a year ago for another woman. His mom hadn't seen his dad since that day.

TJ knew that his mom and dad were not technologically proficient, so participating in a conference call could present challenges for them.

Imagine TJ's surprise when the phone conversation went rather well.

"Hi Mom and Dad."

"Hi TJ."

"Hi Son. Can you speak up? I can barely hear you."

"I'll try Dad."

Two artillery tours in Nam had weakened his dad's hearing but hadn't prevented an inspired high school choir-teaching career.

"I mailed you guys my theater class scrapbook assignment sheet on Monday, with two pictures, the writing directions for each picture, a due date, and a self-addressed envelope for you to send it back to me."

"What's in it?"

"Dad, you should receive it in the mail by tomorrow. Look for an oversized yellow envelope."

"Did you say what's in it yet?"

TJ knew that his dad would not be put off. His dad expected people to respond when he spoke, a carryover from his military days.

"OK, Dad. One of the pictures was taken inside your college music rehearsal hall. You are directing the choir and Mom is playing the piano. The other picture was taken in front of my elementary school on my first day of kindergarten. You and Mom write your thoughts"

"Got it."

"Dad, let me finish. You and Mom write your thoughts, feelings, and details about each picture, anything that comes to mind. I'll worry about my theater professor's writing requirement to create readers' theater picture descriptions."

"Tom, are your hearing aids in?"

"Judy, I have to take them out to hear on the phone."

I think – Mom and Dad are talking again, sort of. "So, Dad and Mom, call me if you don't get the oversized yellow envelope in the mail by tomorrow."

"Call you when I get the mail?"

"That works, Dad."

"Son, did I tell you how proud of you I am?"

"Pretty much all the time, Mom."

"Don't help him get a big head, Judy."

"I can if I want to. It's a mother's prerogative."

"You guys' figure that one out. I need the three of us to meet in two weeks to read over the scrapbook entries to approve them or make additions or deletions. My professor wants them to have authentic integrity."

"Authentic what?"

"Integrity, Dad. It means that to the best of our ability the scrapbook picture details are truthful and accurate."

"Son, I don't know if the three of us getting together is a good idea."

"Mom, we're still a family, even though you and Dad are separated."

"Well, I'm OK with it. Judy, we need to help our son."

"You're right. Where and what time do you want to meet Dad and me?"

"Let's meet at the Sourdough at 4 PM. That accommodates my work schedule."

"I'll put it on the calendar."

"Me too. Mom and you do know that I have to watch my cholesterol?"

"Dad, the cafe has a reduced fat menu."

"Did you say they reduced the menu?"

"Dad, promise me you'll wear your hearing aids at the cafe."

"I promise."

"Well, I gotta go to work. See you in two Saturdays. Love you both."

"Your father and I love you too."

"Call us more often."

"Tom."

"What?"

"TJ already hung up."

"Oh."

## The cafe

Tom had been there before for their memorable engagement moment.

*I thought that the parking lot might be paved by now. Guess not.*

He figured Lowman ordered pavement once a year when the locals got tired of potholes swallowing up tires and spraying rims right and left; figured there wasn't enough extra pavement for a cafe parking lot. He noticed the faded paint on the outside of the cafe building, no doubt due to the restless, unforgiving wind. (thinking out loud) "A new coat of paint would make it look like somebody cares. (Glancing at the cafe sign) At least the illuminated letters on the cafe sign still work."

Tom enters the cafe and goes up to the bar. On the way in, Tom noticed the cafe floor was original, as was the jukebox and pool table. He took note that the ceiling fan wasn't original, nor were the coffee cups hanging from the ceiling like a flock of seagulls taking a siesta. *I wonder if the bathrooms still have red swinging doors.* He pulls out his wallet as he leans toward the red headed bartender, who doesn't look a day over thirty.

"I'd like a pitcher of root beer and three glasses, please." Tom gives the bartender a five-dollar bill. The bartender puts the bill in the cash register, then gives Tom his change. "Does Johnny Johnson still own this place?"

"I don't know a Johnny Johnson."

Tom smiles. "I guess time marches on."

The bartender sets the pitcher of root beer and three glasses down on the bar. "You from around here?"

"Down the road a bit. I brought a special girl here once and popped the question."

"Did she say yes?"

"She did. (pointing to a booth) It was in that booth." Tom takes the pitcher and glasses and sits down in the booth he pointed out. *I am sixty now, but that moment seems like yesterday. We were a cafe couple - Judy, twenty-one, facing me, twenty-two. We each ate a burger and fries and sipped several glasses of root beer; pitched occasional glances at the other while we face-wiped wayward food, and ordered more napkins, again. I* *grabbed the $1.50 bill, while Judy touched up her red lipstick.*

Judy swings her new pickup into a parking spot, opens the door, steps out, and slowly shuts the door. Judy recognizes Tom's car parked next to hers. She feels a bit nervous for a moment, then assures herself "I'll be fine." No matter how hard Judy tried to convince herself to do otherwise earlier in the day, she did at least show up. When she was younger, she would have done the daisy thing. *Maybe it still works.* "He loves me, he loves me no*t.*"

Judy looks around to see if Mary's car is there but doesn't see it. *Mary wasn't that good looking, and she doesn't wear red lipstick.* Lingering by her truck, she imagines Tom's gentle green eyes, thinning gray hair, short and neat, and the permanent marker smile. *I haven't been here for quite a while. The building appears to have aged gracefully. I wonder if Tom will think I have too.* Judy touches up her red lipstick, *just in case,* then, pushing aside the cafe air, she enters.

Tom and Judy see each other simultaneously, his green eyes and her blue eyes locked together in an embrace, culminated by traditional booth chivalry, she sits first, he sits second.

"Hi Tom."

"Hi Judy."

TJ enters the cafe. He was late. His jeans took too much time to dry. TJ had quit smoking, so he no longer needed matches in his tee shirt pocket, though he hadn't completely gotten rid of the habit of reaching for one. TJ is a 30-year-old college senior to be, having given up ranch work three years before to finally get a degree. He is thinking about the three days he's scheduled to spend next week on vacation. TJ slips into the booth, clutching the scrapbook.

"Cheers." Three glasses click together. "Good to see you Mom and Dad."

TJ knew the question was coming. It's usually the first thing his mom asks.

"Are you dating someone?"

"Not really. Finding one like you isn't easy. (pause) Mom, your face is turning red."

"I think it's the glow of my lipstick."

"You look good Son. Working and living here must be agreeing with you."

"It is."

"Did you have a good time at The Haven?"

"That's next week. I did go visit our cabin at Kettle Creek yesterday on my day off. I was opening a cupboard door and decided, for no real reason, to look at the old postcard pinned to it. It's in my pocket actually. (gives it to his mom) Here, you can read it."

"It's postmarked July 6, 1982, and addressed to Sara Parsons, C/O The Haven, 7655 ID-21, Lowman, ID 83637. The note says, Congratulations on your job at the Haven! Love, Mom and Steve."

"So, I'm bringing the postcard with me to see if it's owner still works there."

The Waitress brings napkins and silverware. (smiling) "Are you ready to order?"

"Does the cafe still serve hamburgers and homemade fries? We had that for our engagement dinner."

"Yes, we do. They're my personal favorite."

"We'd like three hamburgers and three large fries." The Waitress leaves to put in the order. The jukebox plays a song.

"Nice day, huh Mom?"

Judy nods, paying close attention to TJ. *He looks so much like his dad did the night he proposed to me.*

TJ picks up the scrapbook and thumbs through it to the first picture drafts, then gives his mom and dad a copy of their own and a copy of each other's.

"The parts are marked by name. There are no quotation marks. Mom, besides reading the parts marked Judy, please read the parts marked for Tom's Mom. Dad, in addition to the parts marked Tom, please read the parts marked for Judy's Dad. I'll read my parts. After both scripts are read for a picture, you and Dad can give any thoughts that come to mind. (pause) Mom, how about you read yours for picture one first."

Judy puts on her reading glasses.

# Judy

Judy: College. Finally. Freeing myself from the plaid seat cover, I finish rolling down the window. Farm air blankets me with fresh cow dung. I feel relaxed. I think it is much like my town, except for the solitary yellow traffic signal installed at Fifth and Main after a boisterous meeting at the barbershop.

*I hear, Did Mable have her calf yet? Does Ted still hog the hay?* I laugh at my stupid thoughts. I know cows can't talk. The Chevy swings into a parking place, a welcome dust relief.

Judy's dad: I guess we can park here. Doesn't say reserved. Don't forget your coat in the back seat.

Judy: I won't forget. Dad clutches my black Samsonite suitcase. He and Mom had bought it as a practical high school graduation present.

Judy's dad: Call Mom and I. Let us know how your money holds up.

Judy: I can feel the let-go sadness. I had felt it before when Dad had to put down my horse, but this is a new feeling. For a moment, I hold on tight, savoring the hug, not looking into Dad's eyes.

Judy's dad: Will you be OK?

Judy: I nod. Take care of Mom. I make a mental note to ask next time about my dog, Blackie, as a warm tear washes my dusty face. Earlier in the car, I had heard the don't quit school for a guy speech. I was ready with my response, though I left the last line out. This is how I rehearsed it in my head: *Dad, I'm here for an education. After graduation, I look forward to putting my college degree to good use. Finding a husband will be a nice bonus.* But this fast? As I turn toward the music hall door, he is standing against the ivy-covered wall, looking quite handsome. I wonder if he jumped out of my U.S. Army poster. *I hope he can't see me blush. It's the kind of blush that causes the don't quit school for a guy speech.*

I pull myself together, hoping I now look like proper girls are supposed to look. He strolls over to me.

Tom: Is this your first day at college?

Judy: Yes. *I wonder how I gave him that idea.* Do I have the word freshman written on my face?

Tom: No, well, maybe a little. I'm Tom.

Judy: I introduce myself. We laugh, awkwardly flirting.

Tom: What is your major?

Judy: English major with a music minor.

Tom: Do you play an instrument or sing?

Judy: I play the piano, but I don't sing.

Tom: I direct the college choir. We need an accompanist. Our last one graduated. We rehearse in a few minutes. Would you be willing to accompany us today?

Judy: *I feel flattered.* I will, but it won't be perfect. *Finding a husband would be a nice bonus.*

TJ grabs the pitcher of root beer. He tops off his mom's glass and his glass.

He grabs his dad's glass and sees it doesn't need a refill yet. "Dad, why don't you microwave your glass of root beer? It's room temperature when you finish it."

"Son, I drink with moderation. Moderation is important."

The waitress brings the food. "Would anyone like dessert brought when you all are finished? We have homemade pie."

Tom looks at the waitress. "It's tempting, but I'd better not." *Why didn't I say that to Mary?*

Judy smiles. "I'd like a piece of pie, warmed up."

"Me too."

"Would anyone like coffee when I bring the pie?"

(Judy, Tom, and TJ in unison) "Yes please." They look at each other and laugh.

"OK. Dad, it's your turn to read."

# Tom

Tom: College. I smile as I think about being a big senior, gladly helping freshman girls find their way around campus. I wonder if I will be the only student from North Dakota, again. Setting that thought aside, I swing into my dorm phone booth, nearly closing the door on myself. We talk about important things first. Then we talk about the other stuff.

Tom's mom: Dad's at church choir, the lettuce and beans are up in the garden, but not the asparagus. Mrs. Adams is hosting pinochle Thursday night, and Sheila has a date with Mike.

Tom: Mom, I have to go now for choir rehearsal. Give everyone a hug for me. Love you.

Tom's mom: We love you too.

Tom: I hang up the phone and head to the music hall. *I probably should have told Mom that my girlfriend, Marla, had called it quits.* I snap out of my thoughts and do a double take. She looks like she is right out of my dad's Vargus Girl poster. She looks stunning and lost. *Maybe I can help her be found.* Finding some initiative, I walk over to her. *She has that freshman coed look.* Hi. I'm Tom.

Judy: I'm Judy.

Tom: Is this your first day here?

Judy: Yes.

Tom: We chat some more. I find out that Judy plays the piano. Choir rehearsal starts in a few minutes. Our accompanist graduated. How about sitting in as our accompanist for rehearsal today?

Judy: OK, but don't expect perfection.

Tom: *Music is safe and more predictable than girls.* I raise the baton. We finish our hamburgers and fries. The waitress brings the pie and pours the coffee.

"So, Mom and Dad, now that you've heard each description of picture 1, any thoughts?"

"I didn't realize I looked like a poster soldier boy."

"I didn't know I was a Vargus Girl."

TJ picks up the scrapbook and thumbs through it to the kindergarten picture; then gives his mom and dad each a copy of their own and a copy of each other's.

"Dad, let's start with yours this time."

"OK. Thank you for making the print large enough for easy reading for Mom and I."

## Tom

Tom: Kindergarten. Finally. I thought this day would never come. Six years of first: first breath, first parent hug and kiss, first doctor checkup.

TJ: I peed on the doctor's tie.

Tom: First cloth diaper, first bath in the kitchen sink, first binky, first time in church.

TJ: My baptism.

Tom: First tooth, first haircut, first restaurant.

TJ: I ate gum off the floor.

Tom: First football throw.

TJ: A spiral.

Tom: First basket.

TJ: On a six-foot hoop so Dad could dunk it.

Tom: First favorite book.

TJ: *There's a monster In My Closet.*

Tom: First Oreos.

TJ: I left some on the white bathroom walls.

Tom: First fish.

TJ: An eight-inch Montana trout.

Tom: First tee-ball hit.

TJ: I tried to run from second back to first base.

Tom: First school outfit.

TJ: Red and white matching shirt and shorts.

Tom: And your first backpack loaded for school. *Going to work will have to wait.* I close the car door and rush inside, in time for TJ's first walk to school; expecting something, but not knowing yet what that might be.

The waitress returns with more coffee. "Mom, let's hear yours."

## Judy

Judy: Kindergarten. Already? This day came too fast. We hang around, none of us wanting to go home. The other moms and dads are here at the fence, watching the children play. The bell rings. Tom and I hug TJ and kiss him. I tell him, Son, have a great first day of school. Kindergarten will be so much fun! Your dad and I will be right here when school gets out to walk you home. The line of twenty-two kindergartners file in.

TJ: I smile as I look back and wave.

Judy: We bravely wave back, holding hands; then walk home, just the two of us now.

Tom: Knowing that some innocence is lost, some wisdom gained.

Judy: And me, a mother with tears in my eyes, keeping our son close to my heart.

Tom and Judy hand their reading sheets back to TJ. He

puts them in his scrapbook; closes it and looks up. Judy rubs her eyes.

TJ thought better of asking for a critique this time. He excused himself and headed for the rest room.

Tom noticed the sadness on Judy's face. "Judy, are you OK?"

"I'll be fine." She wanted to say more but didn't. *What happened to Tom and me? We were so in love.* Tom puts his hand on hers. Judy looks into his green eyes. "You don't have to do that now, Tom."

"I know."

TJ returns to the booth with a pack of matches he grabbed from the bar. He tossed it to his dad. "Dad, do you need a match?"

"No, I quit."

TJ grabs his scrapbook and stands up to leave. "Time for me to be the gas pump attendant. Thanks, Mom and Dad, for being here and helping me with this class assignment. (pause) We talk a lot about relationships in my theatre class. Love can be fragile and unable to survive our stupidity, like in Shakespeare's *Romeo and Juliet*, but fortunately, in real life, we have a chance for a different ending."

Judy reaches across the table to hold Tom's hand as TJ leaves.

"Tom, can I be honest with you?"

"Sure."

"I still love you."

The Cabin

Mom & Dad

Logging Road Hike

Dad Catching some Z's

Dad & Me

The Kitchen

My wife, brother-in-law, and sister with the day's catch.

My brother, sister & brother-in-law – A few years later!

My brother at The Cave fishing hole

My Wife & Me

# PART III - The Calendar

Love ... always perseveres.

1 Corinthians 13: 6

## A little background

Each morning at the cabin at Kettle Creek, the forest darkness gave way to the morning sun. The first one up would start a fire in the cast iron stove, and then the rest would get up when the nighttime chill had melted off their sleeping bags and the coffee pot was percolating. And each morning, a 1951 wall calendar would stare at us as we rolled up our sleeping bags for the day. The calendar month, August, with a penciled note written on it, hadn't been changed.

## The Parsons' home

*Michelle is the 51-year-old widowed mother of Sara.*

*Sara is a 21-year-old college student.*

"Hi Michelle."

"Hi Teri. Thanks for the pictures. I really like how the cabin looks. I think it will be perfect for Sara and me. Thank you for selling it to me. (pause) I got the key in the mail."

Teri shared her story with Michelle. Her first husband was killed in a car wreck when their five girls were really-young – all under the age of ten. Teri couldn't afford daycare. She got behind in her rent payments and she and her girls got evicted. They lived for a short time in the Gospel Rescue Mission. It was there where Teri met Tim, who was helping serve an evening meal.

"He took us in and moved us to Lowman, where we got married. We had our wedding reception at the cabin at Kettle Creek. Unfortunately, Tim had a heart attack last year and passed away. (pause) I wish I could hold him one more time. Because of my Parkinson's, I am moving out of state to live with one of my daughters. (pause) We will always treasure our time at the cabin."

"So sorry for your loss. Please come visit and see the cabin again."

"I will most definitely try."

Sara joins her at the kitchen table with two cups of coffee. "Here's your cup, Mom. I didn't used to, but now I really enjoy our coffee times together."

"So do I. (pause) Is this really my daughter talking?"

"Mom, kids do grow up."

"So, my grown-up daughter, we just bought a cabin."

"Really! Where is it?"

"On Kettle Creek up past the Lowman Southfork Lodge. It's built on forest service leased land and has a forest service outhouse."

"Really? What's it look like?"

"Teri, the previous owner, sent me these pictures. (hands them to her) Sara looks at the pictures. "It looks cute, but rustic. When can we go and see it?"

"How about tomorrow? I think we should stay a week. That still gives you a month before you go back to college."

"OK Mom. I'll start packing. Does it have phone service?" "No."

## The Noble's home

*Steve is the 51-year-old divorced father of Dan.*

*Dan is a 21-year-old college student.*

"Son, when do you go back to college?"

"In a month. (pause) Dad, can you and I spend the next week at the Lowman Southfork Lodge? You promised me some fishing time together."

"You're right. OK, let's pack and leave in the morning. I'll call and reserve a room for us."

"Do the rooms have a phone?"

"No."

## A room in the lodge

"It's what I wanted – clean and reasonably priced; not that I'm a tightwad."

"Right. Hey Dad, I saw a poster in the lobby promoting live music at the lodge bar tomorrow night, August 10, from 9 PM to 1 AM. I'm going to go. You should too. It's time you put yourself out there again."

"You're right. (pause) I never told you, but I went to listen to live music in this bar on another August 10th."

"Really Dad?" What happened?"

"My family and I were staying up the road in a rustic cabin at Kettle Creek that we owned for a few years. There was a really good country band playing that night. I met this girl named Michelle. She looked great in her jeans, red western shirt, and cowgirl boots. When our eyes met, I knew I had to go sit with her."

"Did you – sit with her? You've always been on the shy side."

"I did. Michelle and I stayed till 1 AM. Our favorite song that night was "I Want To Be With You Always" by Lefty Frizzell. I remember giving her a kiss on her cheek, and then I left. I was really dumb not to have gotten her last name and phone number. (pause) I never saw her again. When I got back to the cabin, I took a pencil and wrote "Live music - Southfork Lodge" in the August 10 box of the calendar, to remind me of that special night."

"Dad. You liked her, and you obviously hoped you would see her again."

"I did. (pause) A lot of years have gone by."

"What happened to the calendar?"

"I don't know. Maybe the owners since then have left it on the wall, but I doubt it because it's been 30 years."

"Dad, you said the cabin is a few miles up the road. Can we go see it?"

"Sure, but not the inside since we don't own it."

## The Cabin at Kettle Creek

"Wow. The cabin looks really cool. Do you ever wish you still owned it?"

"Sometimes."

Steve and Dan take the path to the creek. "Kettle Creek is so small and clear. Does it run all year?"

"It does. Let's walk upstream a few yards. Watch out for stinging nettle. I'll show you where we built a dam that produced a little wading area. (points) Wow! Some rocks we placed are still here. It was the only place we had for bathing."

"How long did a bath last?"

"About a minute tops."

"Did you fish Kettle Creek?"

"Lots. We also panned for gold here. We got some flecks over the years, but no nuggets. Let's go see the outhouse and the fire pit."

Dan opened the outhouse door. "Dad, there's a laminated poster of Thoreau in here."

"I can't believe it's still here. It probably wouldn't be here if the hunters didn't like it and if someone hadn't laminated it."

Dan and Steve take the short walk to the outside fire pit.

"A lot of good memories happened here." They sit on a log just outside the fire pit. "I remember singing a few songs with guitar accompaniment.

The craziest one was a country song called Ellie May. I can't remember the verses, but I never forgot the chorus."

"Let me guess, Dad. You're going to sing it for me."

"I am. *Ellie May, my little rosebud,*

*She's OK, she packs a real fine lunch. She knows how to make an old cowboy forget that he's tired and I love her a bunch.*

"Actually, Dad, that was pretty good."

"Should I try for a record contract?"

"No. Can we go fishing now?"

"Absolutely. I'll take you to mom's hole, the cave and the rocks; then we'll stop at the Sourdough for lunch before heading back to the lodge."

"Why is it called mom's hole?"

"It was your mother's favorite fishing spot. I never could get her to try another hole."

Dan leaves a note in the tan box. "I wish Mom hadn't loved meth more than us. It's hard not knowing where she is or if she's even alive."

"I know. She will always be your mom, no matter what. The divorce doesn't change that."

## Mom's hole

"Dad, are we driving or walking?"

"Walking."

The short walk down the cabin road is as scenic as it gets. Kettle Creek flows on the left. Ponderosa Pines reach high to the heavens. Wildflowers abound. So do mosquitoes and deer flies. Just before the road drops down to Highway 21, you can still see what's left of a tree after lightning charred it.

Dan and Steve wait to cross the highway. "Son, the first time I saw this culvert, there was a nice pool in front here. There isn't now. But that day, I saw the biggest rainbow trout I have ever seen in these parts. It had to be at least twenty inches in length. My excitement soon gave way to total disappointment. I couldn't get the fish to hit a worm, a spinner, or a fly. The next morning, it was gone. I never saw it again."

"I believe your story, Dad, but did other people?"

(laughing) "Not many. OK, let's cross the highway and follow the creek to mom's hole. One of the reasons these three holes are such good fishing is that none of them can be seen from the highway. You have to hike to get to them. Not all people want to do that."

They fished there for about 30 minutes. "Dad, that was fun. We each caught and released five. I see why Mom caught so many fish here. Where the creek meets the river is only about two feet deep, but the trout sit there waiting for bugs to come down the creek."

## The cave

"It's just a few minutes hike to the right. We have to hike above the river and back down. The hole is pretty amazing."

Dan saw for himself that his dad had been right. The cave starts as a ripple that flows into and out of a cave on the other side of the river. Dan and his dad caught and released several trout, ten to twelve inches in length, then moved on to the rocks.

## The rocks

Dan and Steve cased the hole from above. Seeing good sized trout ignited their enthusiasm, but the steepness of the  decent delayed fly casting for several minutes.  Cars continually whizzed by thirty feet above them, but they hardly noticed.

"How big was that last fish you released?"

"Sixteen inches."

"That's the biggest one today. What time is it, Dad?"

"It's about lunch time. Let's hike back to the car."

Fifteen minutes later, they were back to the cabin.

"Thanks for going fishing with your dad."

## The cabin at Kettle Creek (the next day)

"Sara, why don't you check the tan box while I use this door key for the first time. Maybe someone left us a note."

"Someone did. The note is dated August 9. It says: What a fantastic place! The Nobles. Doesn't tell what year. (pause) Maybe it was yesterday. Do we know anyone with that last name?"

"I don't think so. Help us remember to leave a note before we leave."

"Glad we brought a high-powered flashlight, Mom. It's really dark in here. How do we open the windows?"

"Teri told me what tools to bring and how to do it." Sunlight broke into the cabin. Sara and Michelle unpacked the car, got their stuff organized, and put wood in the stove and propane in the lanterns. "Mom, there's a lawn dart set here. We'll see who plays better up here in the mountains."

"You're on. Sara, look at these posters – Uncle Sam and a Vargus Girl."

"I bet they've been on this wall for a long time. Mom, did you see the 1951 calendar on the other wall? It's still on the month of August. No one has changed it for 30 years. (Examining it closer) Someone wrote in the August 10 box."

"What did they write?"

"Live music - Southfork Lodge. Who do you think wrote that?"

"I don't know. (pause) I was at the lodge that evening."

"Really? Mom, tell me the story."

"My family and I stayed there that week. That August 10 night, there was live country music in the bar from 9 PM to 1 AM. I met this guy who looked really good in his blue jeans, red cowboy shirt, and cowboy boots. His name was Steve. I never learned his last name or got his phone number. Anyway, when our eyes met, I definitely wanted to sit with him."

"Did you - sit with him?"

"I did. We stayed until the music ended. Our favorite song that night was "I Want To Be With You Always" by Lefty Frizzell. He kissed me on the cheek. Then he was gone. That was it."

"You liked him, Mom. Did you hope that you would see him again?"

"I did. (pause) A lot of years have gone by."

"Does the Southfork Lodge still have live music? Today is Friday. It will give both of us something to do."

"Both of us?"

"Yes, both of us. Mom, it's time you got back out there."

"You're right. Let's head down the highway to the lodge, have dinner, and then see what's happening in the bar."

"OK."

## The lodge bar

Steve and Michelle had been there before. Both were amazed that not much had changed. The bar sign's illuminated letters welcomed them both back. A 1981 calendar, open to August, hung on the wall by the bar entrance.

The band has not started playing. Steve and Dan are already seated at an upfront table to the right of the stage. They do not notice Michelle and Sara taking a seat at an upfront table to the left of the stage.

The waitress takes their drink orders. Sara slips the waitress a note and a quarter, making sure her mom does not notice.

Sara and Dan speak in unison, "Is this what the bar and dance floor was like in 1951?"

Michelle and Steve speak in unison, "Yes."

The jukebox begins to play the song, "I want To Be With You Always" by Lefty Frizzell. Michelle and Steve hear the song being played and rise from their chairs simultaneously. This time, besides a kiss, they exchange last names and phone numbers.

# PART IV - The Postcard

Love ... always hopes.
1 Corinthians 13: 6

## A little background

The Haven Hot Springs is located down the road a bit from the cabin. It is a small motel, adjacent to a restaurant/lounge, small gas pump station, and a hot water pool.

## The front desk

Sara looks down, writing something on a piece of paper. TJ enters through the front door, wearing a backpack. He walks up to the front desk.

"Hi."

Sara looks up from her writing, sees TJ, and says, "Hi." Her blue eyes and his brown eyes met in an embrace. *I have hoped and waited a long time for my special guy. Maybe he is the one.*

*She is beautiful. I hope she isn't dating anyone.*

"I'm TJ."

"I'm Sara."

(handing her the postcard) "Maybe this is yours."

Sara looks at the card. "I haven't seen this card for eight years. How did you get it?"

"It was pinned to the inside of a cupboard door in the cabin at Kettle Creek. My family has owned the cabin for a year now. I saw the postcard every time I opened that cupboard door, but last week, for no apparent reason, I unpinned it and gave it a closer look. It had a name and address, so I decided to see if its owner was still here."

"I must have lost it in the cabin. The cabin owners after us, and before your family, apparently found the postcard and pinned it to the inside of a cupboard door."

"Must have. I'm on vacation for three days. I'd like to spend it here. Do you have a room available?"

"I do. We have a really good country singer playing in the lounge tonight, if you're into that kind of thing."

"I love country music, at least most of it. May I ask you something?"

"Depends."

"Are you single?"

"I am. And you?"

"Yes."

Sara gives TJ the room key.

"Thank you. (summoning up his courage) May I have the pleasure of your company at my table in the lounge this evening? We don't have to call it a date. I'd like to get to know you better."

"I'll be at your table, TJ, but only if it's a date."

"Then, it's a date."

## The lounge

The waitress comes to their table.

"Hi Mandy."

"Hi Sara. Who's your handsome friend?"

"This is TJ."

"Nice to meet you, TJ. Would you guys like another drink from the bar?" "No, I'd like a cup of coffee, black. How about you, TJ?"

"The same please. Do you still serve homemade cherry pie?

"We do. Would you both like a piece?"

"I would."

"Me too, please."

"Warmed up?"

"Yes."

"You told me I would enjoy the hot pool here, and you were right. I took a dip right after I checked in, and it was really relaxing, especially in the cool mountain air. I didn't tell you this earlier, but my parents and I used to come here on some weekend summer vacations. We stayed in the motel. That's how I knew about the homemade cherry pie. Now that we own the cabin on Kettle Creek, Mom and Dad were planning on spending most of their summer vacations there."

"Were?"

"That was before their separation a year ago; now who knows."

"I'm sorry that happened. How are you dealing with it?"

"Better than I was. At first I was really mad at Dad. I couldn't believe he did such a stupid thing, and I told him that. Now that the affair is over, Dad agrees with me. He's told me he wants to make it right with Mom, but Mom wouldn't talk to him until last week."

The waitress brings their order.

(Sara and TJ in unison) "Thank you."

They enjoy the pie and coffee.

"So, TJ, back to your parents. What happened last week?"

"I met them at the Sourdough Lodge Cafe. They were helping me with an assignment for my summer theater class. It was the first time we had been together as a family since the split."

"How did it go?"

"At least they are talking to each other. And Mom held Dad's hand as I left. I think they still love each other, but for them to get back together Mom will have to forgive Dad for the affair. So, we'll see."

The waitress gives Sara and TJ a coffee refill; then clears the pie dishes.

"What about your parents, Sara?"

"My dad passed away when I was very young. I really don't remember him, which makes me sad sometimes. Everyone has a need to know their father, but not everyone gets to. It was really hard on Mom. She balanced a job waiting tables at the Southfork Lodge, which paid minimum wage plus tips, with raising me. We didn't have a lot to live on, (pause) but we had a lot to live for. Faith got us through it. We both love Jesus. Mom taught me we are not promised joy without tribulation, or sunlight without rain. She said we need to give thanks for it all. Now, things are good for Mom. She married Steve, thirty years after they fell for each other in the Southfork Bar."

"What a great love story." (pause) Did you go to school at Lowman?"

"I did. I attended the Lowman one room school. I am one of its proud high school graduates! Mom wanted me to go to college because she never got the chance. I majored in resort hospitality. After graduation, I worked at the Sawtooth Lodge in Grandjean for a summer. It is nestled in the Sawtooth Mountains on land that overlooks the beautiful waters of the South Fork of the Payette River. The lodge rents out cabins and has a restaurant and geothermal pool. Have you been there?"

"I have."

"I liked my work, but it was seasonal. I heard that The Haven was hiring for a front desk position. I interviewed for the job and got it. Hence, the postcard. I have worked and lived at the Haven for eight years. Though the cabin at Kettle Creek is no longer owned by Mom, I frequently spend my days off fishing in the creek or hiking on the logging road. I figured the cabin had a new owner this year because I saw a different car there. I should have knocked on the door. If I had, we probably would have met sooner."

"Do you have plans for tomorrow?"

"It's my day off. How about if we go to the cabin, hang out, and do the logging road hike?"

TJ gets up from his chair. "It's a date. Would you like to dance?"

"I thought you'd never ask."

## The restaurant

TJ was already at a table sipping on a cup of coffee. Sara joined him. "Good morning, Sara."

"Good morning, TJ. I think our first date went well."

"I agree."

Sara smiles. *TJ is assertive, but I like it. I wonder if he will consider doing ordinary things together, like going to the store, taking walks, and doing the laundry, as a date. I hope so. That would be so romantic – a simple way to keep the spark alive through the years.*

Mandy comes to take their order. "Good morning, Sara and TJ. What would you two like for breakfast this morning?" "Bacon, eggs, toast, and a cup of black coffee, please."

"How would you like your eggs?"

"Over Easy."

"And how about you, TJ?"

"The same, please."

The waitress pours their coffee and leaves to put in the order.

"So, TJ, you will graduate with a teaching degree. What do you plan to teach?"

"Government and drama."

"Both?"

"Possibly."

"That's cool. I liked my high school government class, but my favorite class was drama. I was in three school plays. My teacher said I was a good actress, but that was just her opinion. (lost in thought) I would like to be in a play again. I miss it. (pause) FYI, sometimes the Lowman School is looking for a teacher. It is a K-12 school, depending on the grade levels of the students. Usually, they have five to ten high school students. And from a selfish standpoint, if you taught at Lowman, you could use your drama expertise to direct plays. I would try out. I think we could get the community to pool its talent and resources to build its first ever theater playhouse."

The waitress brings their food and refills their coffee. Sara and TJ continue the conversation.

# The logging road

The hike starts at the cabin, wanders several miles up the side of a mountain, crosses Kettle Creek, and finally drops down to the Sourdough Lodge. It is a good hike, full of blooming wildflowers and elk droppings.

"TJ, I love you."

"I love you too."

"TJ, look at this meadow. God says to be still. Maybe doing so is one of the greatest gifts He gave us. Every time I'm here I see something new. Unless you take this hike, you would never know it is here. God is in all of it. Let's just sit here on this rock and take it all in."

While sitting there, the idea of a book about the cabin at Kettle Creek came to Sara. She shared it with TJ. "Not a lot of people get to personally experience the magic of this place, but a book could bring it to them. Our families could facilitate it happening, but the logistics of making that happen could be a challenge."

"Why don't we have a weekend reunion at the cabin at Kettle Creek; get everyone together and talk about the book? The cabin will sleep four comfortably and we can set up a tent or two; we can make the sleeping arrangements work."

Sara and TJ walk back to the cabin, holding hands; enjoying all that the logging road hike has to offer.

# PART V - The Reunion

I know that everything God does

will endure forever; nothing can be

added to it and nothing taken from it.

Ecclesiastes 3: 14

The reunion did happen, but only for six of the eight. Dan and Teri were unable to attend. They all knew that the day would come for them when there would be no more scrabble games under the soft lantern light,

...no more trimming the overgrown bushes that blocked the path to where hands were washed and teeth were brushed,

...no more lawn darts tossed,

...no more dogs chasing a tennis ball down the cabin road,

...no more time spent relaxing in the cabin lounge chairs,

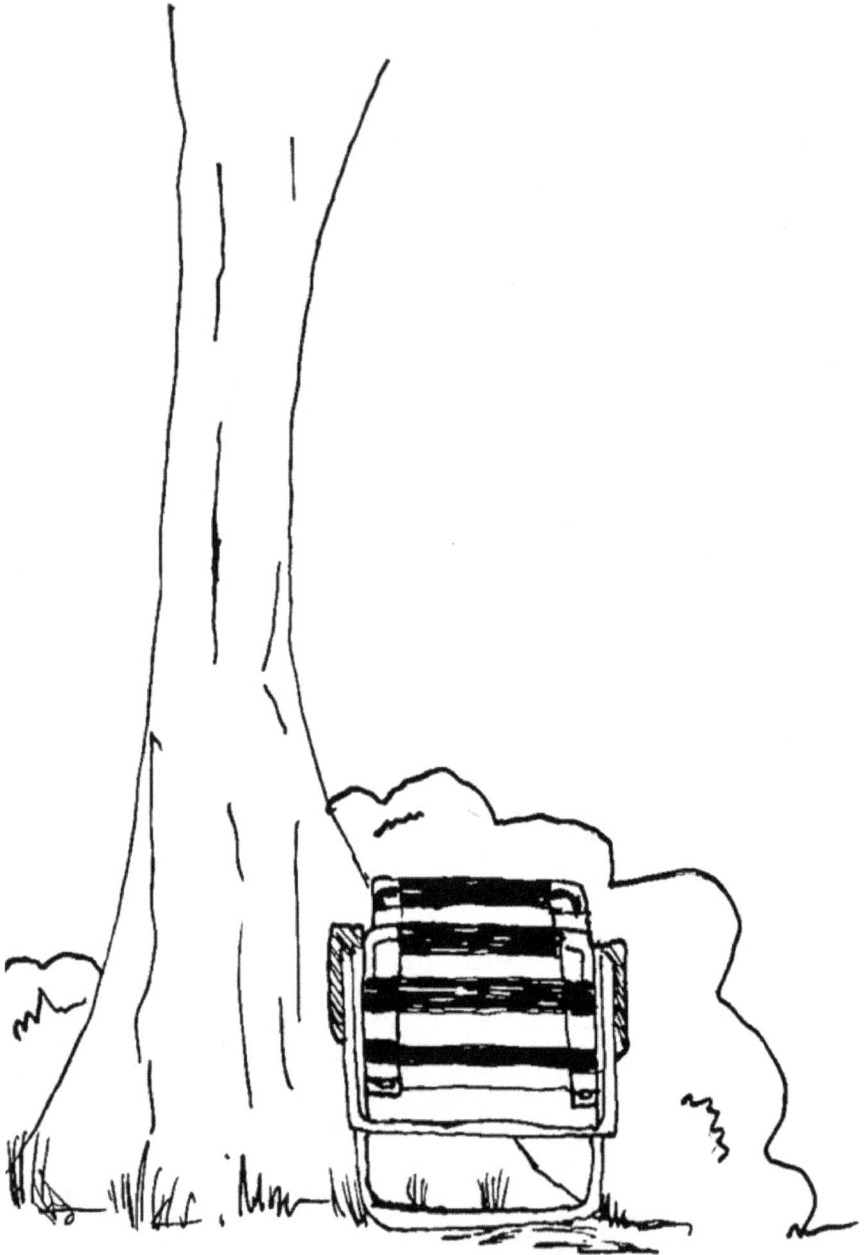

...no more dams to make in Kettle Creek,

...no more cutting wood for the cast iron stove,

...and no more hats hung up on the inside of the cabin door. It will be profoundly missed.

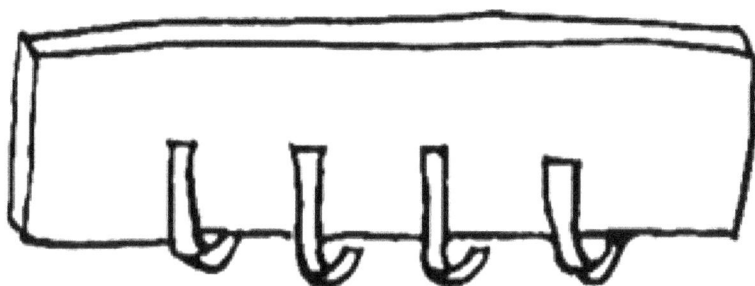

But for now, they enjoy the reunion. There is something about being in a cabin next to a creek in the mountains that makes everything better - food, drink, board games, philanthropy, romance, and books. It was said more than once that weekend that the old percolator on the cast iron stove still made the best hot coffee ever, and that the pancakes cooked in bacon grease were really, really good. Judy won scrabble both nights. TJ and Sara got engaged. All liked the book idea, and they agreed to do a service project to benefit the Lowman community - providing new shoes for students at the Lowman school who need them.

When the weekend ended, they packed up. Everyone signed a penciled note in the tan wooden box by the door.

Then, after taking one last look around, the six reunion members said goodbye to the cabin at Kettle Creek.

On the way home, they did what they had always done. They stopped at the Sourdough and ordered a two-scoop vanilla or chocolate ice cream cone.

When the waitress brought what was ordered, a prayer was said.

"Thank you, Lord, for the ice cream cones, each other, and the cabin at Kettle Creek. Amen."

It would be their closing ceremony. No elaborate banquet was prepared. No awards were presented. No speeches were given, and no media was present. Six ice cream cones and a short prayer: a humble celebration of gratitude so inauspicious it likely went unnoticed by the others who were there. But as the reunion members enjoyed their ice cream cones in the cafe booth that day, if they were listening, they would have heard the angels sing.

# Epilogue

The next summer, TJ and Sara got married in the Lowman Community Church. To no one's surprise, the cabin at Kettle Creek hosted the reception.

Much has happened since then. Steve and Michelle are spending the year traveling across the country in a RV. Tom and Judy renewed their wedding vows. TJ got a teaching job at the Lowman School and is the chairman of the community's fundraising effort to build a theater playhouse. Sara quit her job at the Haven, so she could be a stay-at-home mom of twin girls. Teri no longer makes her annual trip to Lowman because of her Parkinson's. Dan has a girlfriend, though no one has met her yet. And the book that Sara envisioned; it did become a reality. Its author and illustrator hope that you enjoyed reading it.

www.ingramcontent.com/pod-product-compliance
Lightning Source LLC
Chambersburg PA
CBHW050551280326
41933CB00011B/1799